M000286370

FINISHING LINE PRESS
www.finishinglinepress.com

ASSISTED SUICIDE TALK SHOW

poems by

Dan Fecht

Finishing Line Press
Georgetown, Kentucky

ASSISTED SUICIDE TALK SHOW

ISBN 978-1-64662-088-3 First Edition

Publisher: Leah Maines

Editor: Christen Kincaid

Cover Art: Richard Vinson (richardavinson.com)

Front Cover Model: Xavier Perez (xrose.bandcamp.com)

Author Photo: Tainara Fecht

Cover Design: Elizabeth Maines McCleavy

Printed in the USA on acid-free paper.
Order online: www.finishinglinepress.com
also available on amazon.com

Author inquiries and mail orders:
Finishing Line Press
P. O. Box 1626
Georgetown, Kentucky 40324
U. S. A.

Table of Contents

If you or someone you know is having suicidal thoughts, call the National Suicide Prevention Lifeline at 1-800-273-8255

Suicide doesn't take away the pain, it just gives it to someone else.
—unknown

"Transformation is a process, and as life happens there are tons of ups and downs. It's a journey of discovery—there are moments on mountaintops and moments in deep valleys of despair."
—Rick Warren

"There are far, far better things ahead than anything we leave behind."
—C.S. Lewis

"Think of all the beauty still left around you and be happy."
—Anne Frank

This book is dedicated to those who struggle with the issues of mental health and to those who struggle to understand those with mental health issues.
There is a steadfast hope...

THE CELEBRITY

My next guest is contemplating no longer living.

Please welcome the one, the only, the spoken of,
Albeit highly forgotten,
Mr. Cade Burnout!

<Standing ovation>

- Welcome.
- Thanks for having me.
- We'll cut right to the chase.
- That's quite fine.

Legs crossed like a therapist, stain-ridden suit pants,
Charcoal-raggedy tie, blazer tight in the arms, waiting and
Listening for the host to summon sword-like questions from
Dry lips. Water in mug quivers from sound waves.

- So, you've decided you no longer want to live?
- Correct. That's correct.
- But why…die?
- Liberty from the atrocious.
- I see…would you care to share your reasoning?
- Well, it's a long story. Quite long.
- I'm sure everyone would like to know…

<Audience erupts in applause>
<Cade Smiles. The host smiles>

<Camera fades out>

SNAP OUT OF IT

Say it louder for the people in the back!

I solemnly swear that my interest in existence
Has faltered like Icarus plummeting into the Aegean.

Nose-dive. Iplane.

Just break free, they said.

A mental barrier muting the trigger impulses and
The firing of dopamine through my brain.

Confiscate my future.

Snap out of it, they said.

If my mind will change, then Lord speak in my sleep
By way of paralysis in light of an archangel.

Or-
Then I become a fish in the Mariana Trench.
Dark, but I am swimming.
Predators-not seen.
I pray to not be prey.
Sometimes.

A FIGHT INSIDE

The last years have stung,
Which makes sense to only those who throw
Fists at their life. Know-how came but at a loss
Of living, contaminated by voices chanting
Words we don't speak of—Swear words we don't want to hear.

A world only seen through the eyeballs of
A transient son or daughter. A land covered in the leftovers
Of those lucky folks' dinners. All bone,
No meat or substance, what you'd give a dog to
Keep him shut-up for hours
To sharpen his teeth like Japanese forged steel knives.
But sharp teeth mean nothing when there's no fight left inside.

Culmination of self? There's no fight left inside.

CAVE SYNDROME

A cave that has no color.
Ask your tour guide caver where he's at.
No reply because he left.

You see the everyday as pitch-black with a thousand layers of shade.
Like putting silence itself in a soundproof room.
Forget the light even though you know its out there somewhere.
But you like it because that's not living.
Ideal isolation.

Put your hand in front of your face and watch your brain play tricks
Making you believe you can catch the formation of your fingers.
You saw nothing—your brain says otherwise.

SILENT/VACANT

Stillness can be my greatest teacher
Causing me to think for myself
Causing me to lick wounds where the scars subsist
Moving through me enough to cause an inner whirlwind
Silence never bought me any friends
Causing me to speak when most others don't
Causing me to become a teacher with zipped-lips
And now I'll have to state the truth.

This is the space beneath my upper left ribcage
[ ]
Vacant, you see

These are words that never left my tongue
"......"
Silent, right?

Here's my two eyes if I coexist with a hand to hold me down
X X
Gone.

FALL APART IN FRONT OF EVERYONE

Just think; falling apart in front of everyone.

Tell the spectators to sign their names on their notepad to sell their souls for pennies to the banker.

But you've fallen apart, and the room erupts in hard-to-ignore giggles, so hard it splits your sides and you lose your breath—souls have been sold and no one double checked the exchange rate. You forgot to call for Christ to intercede.

Do you call them sell-outs? Do you call them friends? Do you call them betrayers at their best? Fools on full display?

Just think; you can fall apart in front of everyone at anytime, anywhere.

CHILD PERSECUTION

In class, they were raising their hands to spell a word.
Teacher—lips turned upwards.
At this time, you still laughed, until the playground fists were thrown.
Temple—bruised.
Swiftly, you converted from class clown to quiet student.
Speech—lost.
Ah, daydreams of making your oppressor pay.
Tears—running.
Hoping, he'll ignore you while you eat mother's turkey sandwich.
Slap—face.
Bed time, stewing over thoughts of losing sleep.
One—year
Of this, is enough to drive an innocent child away.
From—everything.

FLOAT THROUGH THE CEILING

Cold, hard, laughter is a lesson
For the adolescent,
Empty bodies at desks not ready to learn,
Like being on the outside of access into their tribe,
The new kid, he'd be nice if he wasn't
So quiet, they'd say, with a sendoff of a
Whisper, coarse from ongoing puberty.
The classroom ceiling is more than a
Battlefield of spit wads cemented
Over time; the ceiling is your sky-
Escape from a room full of tiny tyrants, a way
To ascend to heaven then descend to your house
And further descend into your bed, yanking the sheets up
To your chin to weep openly in a room full of
Racecar pictures that mommy and daddy's money
Bought you to keep you pure and candid.
Mommy and daddy don't know you discovered
The lesser thing via means of being yourself,
Leaving a young child to feel their best hours are the
Hours in which they are asleep when rapid eye
Movement is the only recess left.

WE'RE LIVE!

We're back with Cade Burnout. His new book
Assisted Suicide, documents his life from childhood
Up until now and why he is planning on taking his own life.

- So, you fell into depression at a very young age?
- That's right. Too young.
- And you haven't been able to rid yourself of it since?
- If I could then I wouldn't make this decision.
- What about your loved ones?
- Not everyone is meant for love. I never believed when they said that there was someone set aside by God for everyone. Well, I guess I do. But, you know, doesn't matter now.
- You do believe in love, huh?
- No, I don't. Take that back. My time for love passed long ago.

Some in the audience wipe their cheeks. Some in the
Audience tilt their head sideways to better internalize
His words. A woman calls out *Don't do it! Jesus loves you!*
And is promptly escorted out by security, kicking her legs. Some others
Are entertained by the novelty of pre-meditated death.

- Fast forwarding a bit, were there any moments as a teenager that you enjoyed?
- Of course. Plenty.
- Do you ever reminisce of those days?
- Yeah. They were little gems amidst dump truck piles of dirt, though.
- I assume the bad days were…
- …really bad. Makes me sick.
- Would you care to share?

<The audience erupts with applause>

<Camera fades out>

HUDDLE OF FRIENDS

A gateway of testing that you pay for
Over time like life trials. Just a cigarette
Now, to puff with the cool kids, to buy a future
Through nicotine-laden present tense.

You should be laughing. Teachers and counselors drill it
Into your head to not smoke. But what am I to do? Stand
Here in this huddle of friends as the odd man out?
Fourteen and wise beyond my tears.

Like placing my lips around a car exhaust and forging
Good taste. Skin smells of sin (Christ told me
Not to). Are we all friends yet? Can I be a part of the
Clique?

Yes, you're a part of us now.
Virgin lungs fill with new filth.
Oh, you're going places, kid.
Deep-set, sunken eyes are listening.
You're going places you'll never want to go, kid.

BOW YOUR HEAD AND CLOSE YOUR EYES

Sitting in the pews for pastor's preaching about how us people are like
Microwaves with a quick minute option. One button press, done. We
Want everything faster than fast.

Mother's in-tune and father is nodding off, mother poking him.

Shepard speaks.
The sheep listen.
Am I the only one
With restless leg syndrome?
Commandments to be
Followed, seems a
Crushing task for
Teenager.
But I want this
Wholeheartedly.

I wear a watch.
It's a quarter past late.
I set the alarm and
Let it go off as a reminder
To wrap it up.

Elderly woman in Sunday hat
Turns around and scolds me
Your timing is not God's timing!
I didn't understand.
I just wanted lunch.
Oh, double meaning.

GOOD MORNING, AMERICA

Medication severs nerves/
Commercials vending anti-misery pills/
Doctor must see dark cloud revolving around your head/
Writes script/
Now you swig every morning/
Along with organic coffee

> You feel like a mannequin.
> Featureless.
> Phantom Arteries of plastic.
> A heart that isn't there.
> Your personality got left at home
> In an orange bottle
> Child safety proof.

Do not take Funzac if you are taking Exciteozide or Awesomeylene.
Some young people have thoughts about suicide when first taking
An antidepressant. Stay alert to changes in your mood or symptoms.

Make it a great day by...making it a great day (opens bottle).

OUR SACRIFICIAL LAMBS

Dear Journal,

Look at us, ricochets from the Golden State to the Old Dominion in the land of the free, and all the sacrificial lambs of the classroom not ready for looming crucifixion, more

Concerned of sharpening their pencils and honor roll impressions, as the metal door swings and reveals the kid who always wears those gothic skeleton gloves, quoting

A movie *hasta la vista, babies*, and doing next which I shut my eyes and shake my head over, innocent disappearance from earth and to heaven far too soon, they jut under desks

And behind the fish aquarium, which isn't enough when the bullied child plays Nazi Soldier, inspired by daddy's fan club memorabilia, can we say a trigger finger, as

He surveys his new-found hush-quiet in the smoke, your knees rattle beneath the desk, hoping only that you can sob in silence. These children of someone, all the lambs of

Blameless, whose blood is spilled over and over until this crimson atones America of such iniquity, because one day a politician's child could be in class trying to take

Refuge themselves, and if they come home, they'll cry all the cries of the souls that passed before them, or run into daddy's arms, and father will turn in his gun, put on

His suit and march upwards to Capitol Hill to protect these children. Then, you snooze your alarm, eyes wide and bulging, staring at the ceiling, has it all been a prophetic

Dream? Gawking at the gun you hang on the wall for hunting, realizing you have some ugly power, but do you really need it hanging there? A Wicked version of I have a dream.

MAGIC ACT

And that gun that hangs on the wall
Maybe
You learned to like it.

And every day you gazed at that gun
In case
You chose to do it.

Just like a bad magician, make yourself
Disappear.
But then, you can't bring you back.

3, 2, 1

We're talking with Cade Burnout!
His new book, *Assisted Suicide*, talks about what it is like to live
With severe depression and how he's managed it to this point of his life.

- Did you ever look at life as if it were a beautiful thing?
- Yes. Sometimes I still do.
- Then if you've ever viewed it this way, you've likely got some memories tied to it I'd assume?
- Yes, I do. A lot of good thoughts. I really don't want to talk about this. Can we skip this one?
- Would you care to share?
- I don't think so. I've already decided to end things. It's over. No point remembering the good times.
- No point at all?
- No point at—

<The Crowd jeers>

- Cade, I think the audience wants to hear what you have to say.
- Alright. I'll share. Just a little.

<Camera fades out>

BEAUTIFUL CREDENTIALS

In the womb, shortly into this "living" game,
I developed my own divine signature /
These fingerprints are mine,
Barcode and credentials? /
All of the above,
And yes—this too shall last/
My DNA is inscribed like novels,
Making libraries seem as post-it-notes/
And rocket science like long division,
Just to come up with me/
I feel unworthy to be specified such a treasure,
Given to live and affect others' happiness/
And to do with it what I can,
Before the Christ taps his pocket watch with elevated eyebrows/
Perhaps it's a wakeup call to all my intentions,
Sleep is the enemy, son, life is your charity/
I was born to be someone, they say.

ART AND ITS CASUALTIES

Think of all the talent that evades this earth
Before ever being discovered. Lost strokes of a paintbrush,
Words gone unread, songs gone unsung, inventions
Which never left the creator's head. Culture suffers the
Grievance of a myriad of vanished souls that could have
Healed another soul with art.
Have we put too much stock into the almighty dollar?
Some that can't even argue desire law school.
Many who don't even like people consider a doctor's scrub.
Reprimanded at a young age for feeling dissimilar to the crowd,
You have been. You swam like a salmon, upstream and out of dreams.
If you quit, you're a statistic. Demise of the tree you planted.
Soil gone solid. A shrub that wants the shadows. You can only
Wilt, because they tell you to. But those that think outside
Of the box don't worry about walls. This is how talent will
Grace this earth as medication.

LIKE THE SOLDIER DOES…(for Lee T. Jones)

Shouldn't I find a reason to live?
When the soldier sacrifices his
Perfectly livable life for his country
And returns home, having
Inadvertently driven over a roadside bomb,
Thrown thirty feet, on fire for fifteen minutes
with an entree of brain damage,
First-degree burns, heart attacks and
Strokes as the side dish, and a forecast from the
Physicians to not live much longer as a cruel, hard-to-swallow dessert…
Shouldn't I find a reason to live if this soldier
Can recover, smile more than I have ever smiled,
And continue to prove everyone's expectations wrong
With the tender personality of a saint?
Shouldn't I be living my only life like it is my only life?
If only. If only I can soldier through life like the soldier does
When it comes time to soldier on.

PANOPHOBIA OR A FEAR OF EVERYTHING

Disheveled years, but I can't complain, or maybe
I can.

Blaming all those around for the trials you didn't need
That latched on much like a gold rusher gripping his gold

Dust, observing it in a sand timer hourglass with innocuous eyes,
Watching of your youngsters' passing moments,

Not knowing all the young grow old. Of course, I blame
everything for the damage done. Nothing safe. Hinting at "blessed"
tradition trampled into my head by ancients and the lightning bolts from

above striking down those who ramble with the lost.
Maybe I once liked to pal around with those who needed swigs of holy water,

Maybe I broke bread with those too soon taken, maybe I wasn't
Of the come-to-expect church folks. As the cycle

Of households is but a brief eighteen years, reflecting on
The good ol' times we had, us smiling in the specialized

Photographs on the wall. A family tree of many branches. Branches end up
With sub-branches and roots are buried deep. Holy water fed the soil.

WELCOME TO EDEN COUNSELING

Psychologist, Bible or friend
Or how about

Religious-based psychologist
Then ask a friend

Opinions, please, I want
Them all for

Diagnosis of not myself
But of everyone else/

Okay psychiatrist, the
Psychologist let me down

You're my last chance
At a healthy home.

The doctor tells me what
I don't want to hear

Therefore, I'm never going
Back—maybe it's true.

Flip the yellow pages to
Find out who else

Takes your health insurance
With the softest tissues for tears.

Sometimes man can't counsel;
You've got to go into another realm.

SENTIMENTS

Life is full of color
As we toss and turn, trying to
Figure out if we prefer the
Mountains to the ocean.

I always pondered how one
Could favor the plains over
The highest peaks and the
rolling seas.

It must be because of
One's ability to see all around
Themselves, flat and open.
Borderline relaxed.

If the enemy attacks from
Behind, you can't be sidetracked
By the beauty of the peripheral.
Ever imposing on me.

IN REPAIR

Here, my time leaves
As my feet stand on the dirt of earth.
My age versus the ground's, which isn't
One with recent fledgling blooms tangled to a smell
Of a downpour, just one perfume of mother
Nature. I can almost bite the salt in the air and make it
Crunch, how could I not want this?
Tomorrow, the work order will commence to dissect the
Trees I've seen for thirty years, and those who came
Before me for lifetimes. The chainsaws will crank
And the blades will sweep through the bark like a butter
Knife through a fresh flan, all because someone who sits
forever in a sixty-nine-degree air conditioner
fought against a couple branches falling into a backyard.
As you inflict certain harm
On our only constant stage—earth. In repair over many years
before me.

THANKS FOR TUNING IN!

Thanks for tuning in! We're back with Cade Burnout.
His new book, *Assisted Suicide*, is out now, so
Pick up a copy wherever fine books are sold.
The New World Times has called it, "Lovely and introspective. This nihilistically entertaining man puts life on a pedestal and lets the shelf drop on his head from excess heaviness! Poor fellow!"

- Cade, based on what you just shared, you truly have a love for certain things. You can't hide that. That's impossible to hide.
- Well, we as people were born to love in the first place, so maybe now I accept that.
- But, stop me if I'm wrong, won't you miss these little things?
- No.
- C'mon.
- I won't. I've had enough. Quit while I'm behind, I guess.
- But, don't you think you are fighting a mental illness that should be addressed?
- I've been addressing it with my psychiatrist for a while now.
- And quitting is the best thing for you? With all that you can offer?
- Yes, yes, it is.

<The host looks at the audience with a blank face>

Only the sound of a few audience members shuffling in their seats and popcorn dropping to the ground—but you can't even hear that.

A man sneezes and a woman coughs. Plastic bottle drops. Someone burps but no one laughs.

<Camera fades out>

VISITATIONS?

I can't explain it, my feet were just like pillows of feathers
Trampling through the blades of grass dripping with tears
Of the morning dewdrops—you were there in spirit and I chased
You, healthier now that you weren't any longer
Of this Earth—you said to follow yet I couldn't come within an
Arm's length.

- And I ran like the memory of childhood and water balloons
And freeze tag before dinner, too

Like I said, there was no closing in as you hovered above the grass –
But these feather pillow feet of mine were taking flight like the dove
these pillow feathers were plucked from—father, I'm joining you, let's head
straight toward the rising sun and reminisce of all the other birds who
look nothing like us funny-looking airborne individuals!—*no,* you say, *not yet*
for you as you rocket away.

- And I nose dived with the thoughts of adulthood and water bills
And frozen foods for dinner, too

THE RACE

Go on a run in the a.m.
Incense of the air, renewed for another day.
See the garbage bags on neighbor's porches
Which critters ripped into overnight for slops.
Neighbor always waves, and I nod my head.
Head down to never even/ever speak
Yet, in my morning,
The most wondrous thing of all
Is to see a bird flying to race a car
Side by side
With no finish line for either,
Just a stoplight, and then the
Bird wins.

ANY PRESENT MOMENT IS A TREASURE

I loved the lack of the corporate man on the land, the dirt on a child's knee, the grass stains on jeans from roughhousing upon the grass hills of green, fire ant hills we'd avoid in our bare feet, the smell of fire singeing summer chicken over the grates above gray coals as the sun falls below the seven-foot wooden fence that separates my property from yours.

I am watching the bulldozer abolish my house full of memories like a dog's tail across a chess board, minus the growling from the dog but plus the growling from the depths of my soul. My seatbelt tightened—turn the ignition on and speed away.

The trees were all next in line, the ones behind where my house was, taken down as if a tornado had touched down—there's no recognizing this place any longer unless I close my eyes to envision yesteryear coming together to feast at a banquet table buffet full of smell-spooned memories of days when life was full of golden apples and comfort foods.

When I fall asleep tonight, I want to go home.

MISFIT

Bad news. Messengers of the good news don't
    Reside in the mouths of talking heads.
I wake up to hear of Jews and Arabs and
   Christians gashing each
    Other's throats, bombs as background noise
For those "closest" to God, the religious
    Tripping the eternal-life fantastic, counting bodies
Laid in rows on an iphone calculator, video glimpses
    Of holy death played in loops and I can't have
A proper breakfast. I don't belong. Get me outta here.
    Religion ruins love and ruins me.

PRISON ON WHEELS

There's that saying we all detest—something
About *Why do bad things happen to good*
People?

Life committed a flagrant-foul against you, father,
Picked you up by the kitten scruff, in limbo to
The world.

Some of these weapons of war come back to rendezvous
Like an arch nemesis at your door twenty years down
The line.

And you're fading slowly, a fad souring in the minds
Of high school cool kid trends and their aging ways of wannabe
Celebrity.

Give others the good and gain a short stay on earth—spoon feedings
Like an infant for Father's Day dinner. My eyes blister to even
witness.

Sail on your boat, carving through the waves off an Atlantic
Coast which had been attained. Desert storm was not a war
We won. Or you.

This Father's Day is an empty bells and whistles wheelchair taking up space
In a garage, waiting for online bidders to make their best offer. Rid us
Of this prison. Can't go on without you here.

CASUALLY INDIFFERENT

When the most looked-forward to part of your day is bedtime, you're in muddles.
Sleep is like drunken nights—time passing fast to summon no memory.

Now the world is your wax candle, three-fourths molten goo curdling
Down the edges, flame so close to tapping the candelabra, sitting
Stoic on the floor as the weight of heaven and hell battle for dominion
Between your ears.

I feel casually indifferent about everything, you repeat
To everyone you know. No way to put those pants on, one leg at a time.
But what is the passing of the hands on a grandfather clock and how can it be best defined? Do these moments need be filled to the brim? Or is a taste of torment to romanticize? Whatever it is, you need only most of. Less or more.

You know what your spiked ball and chains are. You know how the dog muzzle
Kept your mouth sealed. Today, you'll open the door to sunlight coddled with
Crisp air as the nature greets your morning with a symphony of sounds. Hopefully.

QUASIMODO

I should have listened years ago.
Do you hear me? You'll never hear words like this again…

When you say that you are a zero—
You'll become the exact number. The opposite ringing true.
Waves of words,
more controlling than any of the punches you
Want to throw through fortifications,
shattered knuckles to help
Release. But still, you say that you're quite good at
Always losing, fueled by some music which tatters your
Birthright, poisoning you with an injection of the likelihood of a blank slate,
Straight to the heart to subtract the beating. These words
Command our lives and we animate like everything is a blurred
Day-to-day, somehow put here.

Look at
your neighbor in shadow…head turned down like you, Quasimodo, kicking crickets and blades of grass in muddy Converse all stars. Help her. Speak to her like you've spoken this to yourself. Save without sacrificing a quarter.

Do you hear me? Quasimodo? Do you read me? Quasimodo? Hello? Answer me? Please.

DEPRESSED JESTER

My career feels like:
I give bad news to the king
In a ridiculous way.
Sorrow for my status / woe and gloom
Low spirits / despair
Melancholy / dejected
Blue / depressed
Who am I? / cards in hand
Magic trick / oh, shucks
Lose against myself / No good at games
Jokes / laughter
Hilarity / amusement
Delight / glee
Knee slapping / now high spirits
Hang my hat / back out onto the streets
After work / still a joke
At the bar/ wash the burdens
This is not / my life's anecdote
A round of poison / keeps me amusing
Next day / hat back on
Take the stage / make crude sounds
Wanna play / yes, I'm a clown
Depressed Jester, and there's
No way out.

SPIRITUAL FOOD

I'm in the back pew again—
Young adulthood, kneeling, face to the cushion
Where bottoms have sat for a half-century. Not pleasant.

Dogged-heart but jumbled by the prayers,
The Holy Ghost is moving but I pretend
To be a ghost, hard to read and empty.

Stand up and worship, I'm told, but tossing
my hands up is a crime to myself, sacrifices
die hard in a fledgling cerebellum.

Dancing and jumping and hollering and a joyous
Celebration because it's Sunday and the calls of the
Consecrated have me questioning my being.

She shakes the tambourine in my face as if to gain
A reaction, a fire-starter sort of tactic lost on my
Overall lack of interest in bouncing around.

Clock says two hours left, why is God so problematic
To understand when I show up in my Sunday best
Hoping for glowing face for my work week.

The crowd wants to be fed spiritual-food while I'm
squirming in my seat, passing the offering plate, I
drop two quarters in—it's all I have. God, please bless me.

I treat God like a wishing well while everyone else gives
More to Jesus than I can. The shepherd does have a sheep
In me, but please don't pull the wool over my eyes.

Am I a friend of God? Am I a friend of God? Am I a friend
Of God? He calls me acquaintance. He says he will spit me
Out if I am lukewarm. So—start a fire inside or just burn me alive then.

THANKS FOR STAYING TUNED!

Thanks for staying with us! Cade Burnout has come out with a book, *Assisted Suicide*, documenting his decision to leave the earth. And people are L-O-V-I-N-G it!

Cade nods. Sips his water and sets the black mug back down on the desk. Runs his hand through his short, black hair.

- So, I understand that you're a big fan of nature?
- That'd be correct.
- Does that mean you like plants, flowers, or whatever?
- No, more like, I just love being outdoors. Love parks.
- What is it about parks that you love?
- The peace. Definitely the peace and quiet. And the wildlife. Animals that have no priorities or demands to meet. I used to wish I were a squirrel. Collect a nut, climb a tree, go to sleep, rip open someone's plastic trash bag and find a tater tot.

<The audience chuckles>

- Speaking of wildlife, won't you miss it?

Cade closes his eyelids and rubs them with his thumb and forefinger.

- Why do you have to ask this question?
- Because, Cade, we want to know why you want to kill yourself.
- Well, you offered my family mon…

(The host whispers something)

(The host clears his throat)

- Cade, we want to know why you want to kill yourself.
- Look, you're going to make me cry here.

Cade takes a moment. Grabs a tissue he doesn't have time to use.

- I used to pray to God when I was in the nature. I must avoid nature anymore.
- Why? Because you love it?
- Yes.

<Camera fades out>

PORTRAYAL OF LIFE AS A TREE IN THE FRONT YARD

Trees speak with their limbs and branches
Shuddering in a light gust or a stout wind.
To wave goodbye or hello to the people
Like us that live below.
But these trees, you see, they grow anywhere
They wish. They don't discriminate on the town
Or the emotions of the souls of the people
In the homes beneath them.
They are firm yet weathered, elemental and
Essential, cultured by the varying clouds in
The sky above them and the fickle squirrels within
Them. Again, trees don't care of your humanoid
Struggles under your roofs. They continue to grow,
Mature and live on. So, do you wither in your own
Personal winds or act as a tree?

BRAND NEW HOME

A hermit crab traverses the sands
Of driftwood
On a beach of sea debris.
Crab has a new shell; old root beer soda cap

A DAY HIKE

A day hike. But I find dirty trails I've paved in my ten-year-old
tan boots. They say to never hike solo. They say a lot of
things.

I marked the evergreen tree bark with my pocket knife
Twenty years ago, carving some cliché initials of our
Love deep enough to find sap, as if I were trying to harm
The cedar and scar it for life. To injure a tree.

Late afternoon brittle air reacts like a flavor when I open my
Mouth. Red evening from the sun versus the clouds. I've
Not once had to duke it out with a mountain lion in a forest. We'd be
Friends. I bet we would. If not, then I'd be victorious.

This earth is my land and it is your land, too, for however many
Years we get. Then we pass it on like fathers to their sons, from wrinkled
Fingers to unadulterated fingers.
"Here. My treat. The earth."

LEGEND HAS IT

A cardinal flew into my kitchen window. At full speed.
Aerial avian concussion. The bird drops, forgetting
How to fly, seeing stars. Startled and wobbly, faint of bird-heart.

I must become a minuteman veterinarian. Instantaneously.

Legend has it a bird flying into your window means
Someone close to you may pass soon.

I open my door to assist the crippled. It staggers away.
Opens its wings and now airborne. My eyes lose trace
Of crinkled feathers. A bird, bearer of bad news.

SELF EXPOSÉ

Those who do everything for others
Too often
May not do anything for themselves.

RETURN FROM COMMERCIAL

Welcome back, folks! We're back with our favorite vacuum salesperson, also known as the ever-underrated and newly-suicidal, Cade Burnout!

<Applause>

- Now, Cade, we've been talking to you for a bit now.
- Uh-huh.
- And even after all this talk, do you really want to…
- Yep, I wanna die.
- How do you plan to end your life?
- Well, my doctor will prescribe me a barbiturate.
- That might be a hard pill to swallow!

<Audience laughter>

- On a serious note, are you looking forward to that day?
- Yes and no.
- Why?
- Yes, because life has lost its luster and no because, well, the unknown is…unknown.
- The unknown, as in, life after death?
- Yeah.
- Scared there's a heaven or hell?
- You bet.
- So, what if God judges you for all of your sins before the pearly gates?
- Well I won't deny them.
- Do you think God will call you a murderer for taking your own life?
- Of course.
- So, will there be paradise for you?
- I'm not sure. I might need to get myself ready for the broiler room instead.

<Audience laughter, half of audience stays somber and pale>

- Bad joke, Cade!
- I know. But I'm not lying.

NIGHT WINDS

My final visit to the beach and I grasp people are like grains of sand, so many of us to be blown around and stepped upon by the people escaping themselves.

I'm about to escape for good. Work, gone. Beach, gone. Night. It's always five degrees cooler on the beach. Flawless evening to stroll and scarcely see the sea.

North Star is so bright that I nearly have faith in swimming a few miles to reach it. Perhaps I can die trying that rather than a visit to the doctor. It's the effort.

It'd be dark, and none would know I backstroked to my drowning. My eyes would be watching the North Star as I cut through the waves, hands cupped. Water overtakes.

I snap out of it. The elements of ocean air in my mouth and through my hair. Your condos on the beach could be but an audience to my vanishing.

PARTING WORDS

Seismic activity below the surface of my epidermis.
Expiration day t -minus two days.
So far away from God, yet we're soon to shake hands—briefly.
Phone calls can roll to voicemail.
I'm past the farewells and opinions.
Cleft tongues can't comprehend.
Lashing vocabulary—I only see vacant mouth.
Remove my sunglasses as I drive.
The colors of the world, grass is greener,
keeping up with the Joneses, hands
Held on the street, the quickness of the mailman delivering, dogs
Barking behind a wood fence, food that comforts the
Soul, twigs that crunch underfoot, smoke swaying in the
Autumn air, cloudless afternoons, fruits from a tree
Branch, earthy perfume after rain, the effervescent smile
Of love, and every microfiber of my being as
I must kiss these things not goodnight, but goodbye.
Jesus Christ, tell me, what have I decided?

LAST WILL AND TESTAMENT

I, Cade Burnout, being of full age and sound mind and memory, do make, publish and declare this to be my Last Will and Testament.

Give all my possessions
 To my cat.
  He's been there to lick my wounds regardless.

My savings account,
 To my dog.
  Her canines wont grind if others spend her money.

Any debt I still owe,
 To my family
  They'll pay it back for me.

Donate my house
 To a charity
  Which supports fighting depression.

Donate my body
 To furthering science
  So medical students can diagnose my madness.

Donate my brain
 To a Ku Klux Klan chapter
  So they can lust over thinking differently.

I'VE BEEN THINKING

I.

My psychiatrist doesn't like to have appointments with me. Considering, this time we're in the home stretch. Inflated words of empathy fall victim to a concern of which I bludgeon and shoot down as if the Red Baron were in control of emotions here. Throw me every compliment in the book, doc, see if I budge. I budge for no one—I'm like a monk that sets himself on fire in protest. Sit still and scorch. Mind over matter, the matter of your words and talk of consequence. You don't matter. My decision only. Drop the pen pad, sir, there's nothing left to record here. My ball point pen of life ran dry long ago.

II.

Take me back in time a little bit. Before death was my only deliverance from self-proclaimed doomsday. Before loss was a gray cloud that showed up on a regular basis in my house just above my head like a downpour threatening to monsoon upon my every existential quantity of self. Before the wind wanted to take a relic of me with it as it ventured out to sea in the darkest of nights, collapsing someplace in the Atlantic open air
Creating a storm front of epic proportions only to rain down in repercussion upon people who have-not on lone islands. I never wanted any of this in my life. But then it became a friend. But then it became an enemy. But then it fooled me into friendship. But then it was my antagonist. And then it was the perfect embodiment of Satan; my depression. We aren't friends. But I allowed it to ride shotgun.

III.

You're not even homeless, you're not even broke, you're not even an orphan, you're not even sick, you're not even a criminal, you're just a lost child in the body of a man who can't seem to organize their emotions. Oh, aren't you ever losing out! This is life and you don't get it again. You've got it better than you think-you could have been born in Sierra Leone begging for a spoonful of rice and a side of clay playing tug of war over a banana and watching your infant brother die in mother's dirty arms. What's a cup full of clean water? Oh, right, you drink that every day, yet you want to kill yourself. "How mature"...said the psychiatrist after admitting this was a man to man conversation. Anything professional was left behind.

IV.

Disengage myself from everything around me. I am a floating vessel in maritime of desolation. Soon my soul will satellite the orbit of Saturn's rings while staring down on all of creation. No certainty about getting my wings. What if taking my own life breaks the command thou shalt not kill? Guilty for the murder of me. It's payback time in hell. Do I not fear such? Oh, just stop the discomfort.

V.

Too late. If only. Please clap for me. Oh well.

DINNER, SOLO

Pasta dinner. Farewell pasta.
Ziti on my tongue.
Oregano excites my taste buds.
Thank you, parmesan cheese for being
There when I needed you most.
Garlic bread soggy from marinara bath.
One forkful closer to empty bowl.
Empty bowl.
I put my fork and knife down
And skip the dishes.
I lick my bowl clean.
Clean dish.

ORANGE BOTTLE BLUES

They call my last name.
There is a lady checking her blood pressure.
Prescription in a bag.
Mine. Pay. Walk.
Leave the drugstore door and
The alarm goes off.
Warning. Is that a warning to
Me?
Cashier checks my purchase.
Tells me I'm good.
Walk to my car.
In my hand is the end of the world.
In an orange bottle is the key
To another dimension.
Unlock car door with remote.
Rain starts falling.
Thunder starts creaking.
Will I ever see the sun one
Last time?

LEVITATE

I'm between this creation and the next,
As it feels with the lights on, dimly lit,
In a downtown area dancing with
Flickers of spotlights. Once upon a strife,
I worked and lunched here every day.

I'm going to lay on this cement ground,
Until I rise like evaporation to the nightfall
Sky and become a rain melody that the
Amazonian Indigenous pray and dance
for to shower down upon their dirty skin. I want
to be your clean water.

I feel so close to Yahweh. Feel my body lifting.
Escalation. Take me! This world was built for
Fighters and fakes! I am none, just done! I hover
briefly. And drop. What?

MY FINALE

Instrumental violin playing on my bedroom stereo,
Low volume, just enough to set the mood at melancholy,
Drop the blinds and close the drapes
And have a seat on my bed as I unscrew the lid
To the orange bottle.

So many of my heroes have taken their own lives,
I want to be them, have something in common.
Will we shake hands or will they slap me on the head?

I dump the pill into my hand as I look to my ceiling,
The same ceiling, I often see myself melting through
In some sort of out-of-body experience.

Let's make this real.

Goodbye note on my nightstand. Check.

I place the pill between my front teeth, a light bite, balanced in
Place, just to feel myself teetering between life and death.

I saw my life flash before my eyes—childhood—its real—
You do see these things at the end—I'm a drama movie—

Hold the pill steady by my incisors. I am about to cock my
Head back and gulp. Whiplash.

My stereo suddenly changes to "All You Need Is Love", dog and
Cat sit at attention in the doorway, perched, eyeing me like tuna and chicken.

A pill, so very unlike the communion bread—which this will only take from
Me. Nothing to gain.

The room is cold and dry, the light of the room is perkier than ever,
How can I describe a song which makes the room feel noiseless?
The chorus keeps telling me all you need is love. Love, love, love Is
All you need.

I spit the pill into the trash. Dog and cat hop onto my lap. I reach for the Trash, one last chance, dog nibbles my finger like chew toy, as to say leave it Behind in the depths of hell.

THE SHOW MUST GO ON

A knock on my door. "They" expected me to have done the duty.
A yearning for fate has dissipated. I'm alive. I'm alive? I'm alive!

- Hello? Cade? You dead yet?
- I'm alive!

(The sounds of a film crew hiking upstairs, many feet, stairs creaking)

- Cade?
- I'm alive!

The show host swings the door open like a prison guard, the show has gone awry!

- Cade, the deal was for you to kill yourself. Don't make a fool out of me.
- I had a change of heart.
- Like I said, we had a deal. You know that.
- Well, God opened my eyes at the eleventh hour.
- No, no. That's not how the show goes, Cade. (He knocks a lamp to the floor)
- It's my life and I make the rules.
- No, it's my show and I make the rules! Do you understand?

(The camera is rolling in Cade's face, breathing fretfully)

Cade wrestles with the host on the bed. The host gets behind him, splitting his expensive dress pants, headlock for a potential takedown. Cade feels air passages cutting off, and the jugular vein losing current, vision slowly diminishing, tongue hanging for a sense of taste of death in the air.

- If you don't kill yourself then I'll do it for you, buddy! I've always wanted to do this!

(The audience back at the studio stands to their feet, gasping)

Cade is fading. There's no fight left inside. Culmination of self? There IS FIGHT LEFT INSIDE!

Cade shoves the host off him, and the host bangs his head onto the corner of a nightstand. A bloody gash. Junior concussion. Seeing stars.

- Cade, what are you doing? We had a deal!
- I make no deals with you. I don't make deals with you.

(The audience back at the studio breaks into a standing applause)

(The camera crew continues to film in the bedroom. They don't care. They're paid hourly)

The show host stands up and flings the paper scripts to the floor.

- Fool! You changed my plan for your life! I have millions watching! Don't mess me around, Cade!
- There are bigger plans for me. And you aren't part of it.

(Cade tosses an empty coffee cup from his nightstand, bullseye to the temple of the host)

The host drops to his knees and rubs the bruise madly.

- I've got my own plans now. Get behind me, Satan!

The host and the camera crew evaporate into the bedroom's air. The studio audience erupt into a joy not often attainable.

Cade laughs. Then cries. Then dances and praises. Then checks his voicemails. Then washes his dishes. Then quits his job. Then reignites passions. This is a new life. This is what a new life feels like.

New life has been found.

Acknowledgement:

Thank you to the following journals/magazines for first publishing these poems:

The Remembered Arts Journal: "Art and its Casualties"
Plum Tree Tavern: "Brand New Home"

I can't do a good job at expressing my thankfulness. It's too deep. As a student and resident of the world, I can best express thanks to those who have come and gone throughout my lifetime, whose names and faces have become history but unforgotten, who have showed me what poetry and writing was all about without realizing they were ever showing me. That's just life when you pay attention and remain cognizant to the charm of it all.

I thank my loving and effervescent wife, Tainara Fecht, for believing in me from the start, by years ago telling me to "just get myself out there". Reader, I encourage you to not think twice about getting yourself out there. Whatever your field of expertise, it is certainly yours for the taking. Know this.

I thank my American and Brazilian family—Sally, Joseph, Sarah, Ethan, Laci, Roberto, Naiara, and the rest of the family in scattered places throughout the US and Brazil.

Big thanks to Eugene O. Smith and Gigi Smith for your undying sense of confidence in me. It means so much. Imal Wagner for your unbelievable guiding eye. Donna "Dude" Borst for joining the ride as my literary Godmother. Barrett Porter for your casual indifference and lyrical everyday speech. Richard Vinson for sharing your gift of photography with me and more since the days of Seoul. Felipe Hasegawa, we know the journey is young. And to all my English as a Second Language students. Thank you! Obrigado! Any other friends please feel free to write your name here ______________ and I'll call it official!

Of course, I thank every reader who believes in the power of poetry. I thank you for taking time out of your life to read what I have written. I thank you for your word-of-mouth promotion. My gratitude to you is great and may countless blessings overflow into your life.

Furthermore, I thank Jesus Christ, for doing in me what I never thought could be done.

Dan Fecht is Editor of Culture at *DC Life Magazine* in Washington, DC where he writes about society, travel, art, food and entertainment. With DC Life, he also instituted the column "Poet's Viewpoint". He is co-founder, along with his wife, of an English school in Florida and is likewise passionate about teaching conversational English to immigrants seeking a new life in America.

CPSIA information can be obtained
at www.ICGtesting.com
Printed in the USA
JSHW012004091219
2879JS00004B/16